The Renaissance Painters

COLORING BOOK

With paintings selected and redrawn

by Andy Nelson

Culpepper Press
MINNEAPOLIS

A Note to Parents, Grandparents, Teachers and Friends of Children . . .

A child whose activities are directed with loving encouragement, whose experiments are designed to succeed more often than fail, will develop greater self-esteem, creativity, and stick-to-it-tiveness than will the unguided child left alone to his or her frustrations.

Here's how you can help your child make the most of *The Renaissance Painters Coloring Book*:

1. Read the introduction, so you can answer the basic questions your child may ask about Renaissance painters.
2. If possible, present this book in person to the child, explaining that these are pictures of some of the most famous paintings in the world. Browse through the pages with the child, discussing the images, asking which he or she wishes to color first. Read the titles to the child. Note the historical information and offer your own ideas to encourage original drawings by your child on the blank left hand pages.
3. If your child wishes to copy or trace, don't panic. That's a natural and necessary step in the advancement of your child's own creative skills and confidence. In fact, copying was the primary method of instruction practiced by aspiring young artists during the Renaissance.
4. Ask your child, "Would you like me to color with you?"
5. Provide crayons and suggest other tools: colored pencils, fine point non-toxic markers, watercolor paints. Take a moment to show the distinctive marks that each tool makes. Show how to care for these tools.
6. Don't criticize what appears to be messy or nonsensical coloring. Allow your child's self-expression and personal color choices. Our purpose is not to produce exquisitely colored refrigerator decorations but to stimulate your child's imagination through an introduction to the images of some very famous artists. Allow the child to develop that interest in the direction and to the extent he or she desires.
7. To encourage your child's interest in Renaissance art, arrange a trip to the local library or nearest museum. If possible, find and compare full-color reproductions of the paintings shown on the pages of this coloring book.
8. As your child grows, follow up this introduction to Renaissance painters with other appropriate and complementary gifts and books. From such attention and childhood experiences grow fond memories and personal histories.

—Andy Nelson

About the author:

Andy Nelson is the author/illustrator of Culpepper Press's highly acclaimed series of educational coloring books, a series which includes *The Impressionists Coloring Book* and *The Carl Larsson Coloring Book*. He also illustrated Culpepper's children's book, *A Is For At Bat: A Baseball Primer*. He is the illustrator for *The Minneapolis Review of Baseball* and the *Hungry Mind Review*, and is also a mural artist. A native of McIntosh and Winger, Minnesota, Andy is a former public school art teacher and weekly newspaper editor. He has two daughters and lives in St. Paul, where he works on forthcoming children's books.

For my mother, Jeannette Nelson, 1935–1990. And for my favorite Italians: the Joe and Barb DiMaggio family of Erskine, Minnesota and the Tom and Kathy Palma family of St. Paul.

My thanks to Eugene Dalzotto, my art history professor at Bemidji State University, 1974–1978.

Cover painting: *Mona Lisa* by Leonardo da Vinci, reproduced with permission of the Louvre, Paris.
Title page: Two figures from Giorgione's *The Virgin with St. Liberale and St. Francis*, Castelfranco Cathedral.

ISBN 0-929636-10-4 10 9 8 7 6 5 4 3 2 1

CULPEPPER PRESS, 2901 Fourth Street S.E., Minneapolis, Minnesota 55414

Culpepper Press books are available to organizations at quantity discounts.
Write for information.

Introduction to the Renaissance Painters

EVERYDAY LIFE DURING THE RENAISSANCE

In 1347, the bubonic plague swept into Sicily. Within thirty years, it killed two out of every five persons in the world and ended two centuries of steady economic growth in Europe. Yet, in the midst of this black death arose one of the golden ages of art and intellect. The *Renaissance* was an artistic, literary, and scientific revival that began in Italy in the 14th century and influenced the rest of Western culture over the next two centuries.

But, besides the devastation of the plague, life was not golden for the vast majority of people living at that time. Men still were loyal subjects of rich landowners rather than free citizens of the state, women still were not taught to read and write unless they were destined for nunhood, and the majority of people were still poor.

In Florence, for example, in the year 1500, the population of 70,000 was divided into three distinct social classes: (1) the *ricchi* and *uomini savi* (the rich, wise, and powerful old families of banking and commerce); (2) the *mezzani* or *populari* (the commoners– small property owners, shopkeepers, tradesmen, lawyers, teachers, civil servants, and artists); and (3) the *poveri* (the poor masses, socially invisible). The *poveri*, three-fourths of the population, included servants, slaves, builders, apprentices, journeymen, and the labor force needed to maintain they city's main industry, cloth manufacturing.

Despite the desperate life of those at the bottom of the social heap, the emergence of rich merchants and bankers favored the development of the Renaissance. Their wealth made secular patronage of the arts and sciences possible. In the past, the church had been the sole patron of the arts and it certainly continued to benefit–most artists still portrayed religious subjects–but the new art served the added purpose of justifying wealthy patrons' oftentimes precarious claims to power.

Although the Italian Wars (1494–1559) increased political instability, they also spread Renaissance ideas throughout the rest of Europe.

LIVES OF THE RENAISSANCE ARTISTS

Giorgio Vasari, who published *Lives of the Artists* in 1550, divided Renaissance art into three periods:

Pre-Renaissance. Late 13th–early 14th century Italian artists such as Cimabue, Duccio, and Giotto were the "first glimmer of excellence after the dark Middle Ages."

Early Renaissance. The "tremendous overall advances" of painters such as Masaccio, Uccello, Filippo Lippi, and Botticelli combined more careful composition, lighter colors, and more charming and realistic portray als of nature.

High Renaissance. The "Golden Age" led by Leonardo, Michelangelo, and Raphael, from 1475 to 1550.

Most Renaissance artists came from lowerclass families. All began as child apprentices sent away from home to live in the studio of a master artist, where they received several years of grueling training. Once they themselves attained the status of master artist, most opened their own studios to accept the next generation of young apprentices.

To disassociate themselves from the Medieval darkness immediately preceding them, Renaissance artists and scholars deliberately looked to the ancient Greeks and Romans for inspiration. They also began to depict nature, especially the human body, more accurately than ever before–but with a much greater emphasis on ideals of beauty and harmony due in part to the growing acceptance of humanistic thinking. Medieval culture had been church-centered but Renaissance culture was based on the supremacy of personality and the importance of the individual–a radical new attitude more often promoted in art than in politics. Still, art-making came to be regarded as a noble and intellectual profession, instead of the simple craft it had been. Most of the artists in this book became wealthy and famous because of their commissions from popes, royalty, and nobility.

The single most important visual advance in art history came around 1420 in Florence: the development of *perspective* by the architect Brunelleschi, the sculptor Donatello, and the painters Masaccio and Uccello. "Perspective"–from the Latin *per* ("through") and *specere* ("to look")–means that objects in a painting have the same *relative* size, shape and position they would have in actual space when viewed from a single viewpoint–or *perspective*. Simple sounding, but not easy to achieve.

Another necessary skill of Renaissance painters was the ability to accurately depict the human body. Since no woman, whatever her social status, would dare claim a firsthand understanding of the naked male body, there were no female artists at this time. In fact, women remained excluded from all craft professions.

CONTEMPORARIES OF THE RENAISSANCE PAINTERS

Famous people living at the time of the Renaissance included Shakespeare, Henry VIII, Martin Luther, Joan of Arc, Copernicus, Galileo, Saints Francis Xavier and Ignatius Loyola, John Calvin, Machiavelli, Wycliffe, Tyndale, and Vasco da Gama. Famous contemporary artists included Jan Van Eyck, Albrecht Dürer, Hans Holbein, Bosch, Brueghel, and El Greco. (Rembrandt was not born until 1609.)

Meanwhile, between 1492 and 1576, Columbus discovered North America, Amerigo Vespucci discovered South America, and Ponce de Leon discovered Florida; de Soto reached the Mississippi, Cabrillo reached the Pacific, Drake docked in what would become San Francisco, and Henry Hudson sought the Northwest Passage. Within fifty years of the Renaissance, John Smith met Pocahontas, the Pilgrims landed at Plymouth Rock, and Europeans purchased Manhattan from the Indians.

– *Andy Nelson*

CIMABUE (Giovanni Cimabue, c. 1240–1302)

Santa Trinita Madonna

Often truant from school so he could watch Greek artists at work in Florence, Cimabue bridged the gap between Byzantine and Renaissance art and became very rich, famous—and very arrogant. He was Dante's friend and Giotto's teacher.

DUCCIO (Duccio de Buoninsegna, c. 1255–1319)

The Virgin and Child

This is the central panel of a triptych and has been referred to as "The Green Madonna." It was painted in fast-drying egg tempera on wood in about 1300. Even though it's nearly 700 years old, it can be seen in London's National Gallery. It's only 16x24 inches.

Duccio

The Temptation of Christ

Once part of Duccio's masterpiece, the great altar for the Cathedral of Siena, this painting is now part of the Frick Collection in New York. Duccio's personality was far less flamboyant than that of Cimabue or Giotto.

Giotto (c. 1276–1336)

The Flight into Egypt

The son of goat-herders, Giotto achieved tremendous fame. People marveled at his ability to capture such realistic gestures and attitudes. A witty and joking man, he became Dante's close friend and is considered the "grandfather" of Renaissance artists.

FRA ANGELICA (Fra Giovanni Angelica, c. 1387–1455)

San Domenico Annunciation (detail)

Fra Angelica was an equally gifted painter, illuminator, and priest. His name meant "brother angelic." He was a modest and peacable man; lowly, yet the friend of many popes. He could have become wealthy and powerful but that did not interest him.

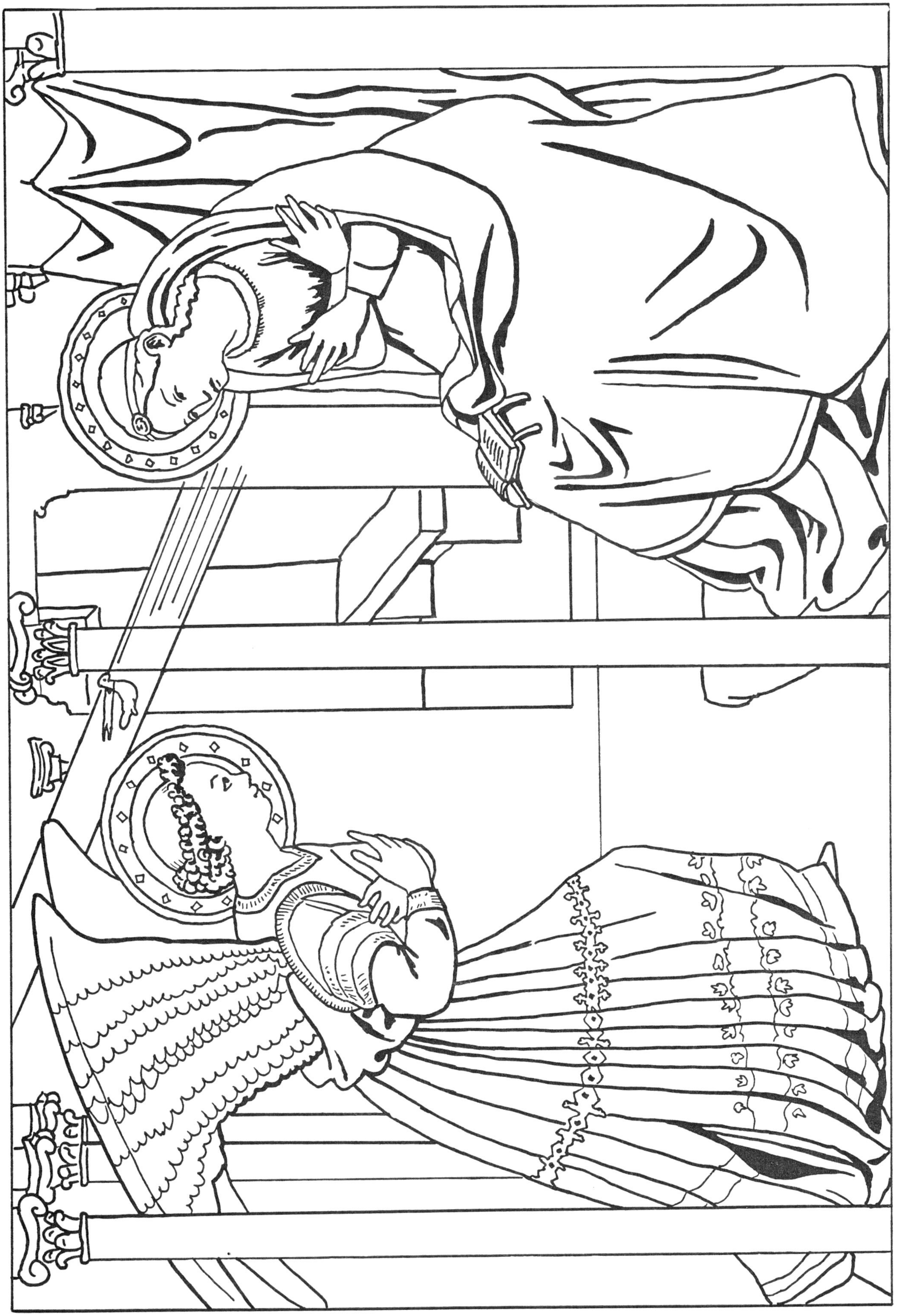

UCCELLO (Paulo di Doni Uccello, c. 1397–1475)

St. George and the Dragon

An eccentric and melancholy man, Uccello is said to have developed an odd psychological aversion to cheese. One of his few friends was the sculptor Donatello, whose gentle teasing unintentionally humiliated Uccelo so much that the painter became a hermit.

Uccello

Battle of San Romano (detail)

Uccello's obsession with the study of perspective kept him from ever properly developing the figures in his paintings and, according to his wife, filled all the days and nights of his reclusive life until he died at the age of eighty-four.

PISANELLO (Antonio di Puccio Pisano, c. 1397–1450)

Portrait of a Princess of a House of Este

Pisanello was considered the greatest medal maker of the Renaissance. He studied in the studios of Donatello and Uccello and was Masacchio's friend. If you go to Paris and see Leonardo's *Mona Lisa* in the Louvre, you will also see this painting.

Masaccio (Tommaso Guidi, 1401–1428)

Expulsion of Adam and Eve

A kind but absent-minded son of a poor notary, whose nickname—Masaccio—meant "Silly Billy" or "Sloppy Tom," this artist taught Filippo Lippi and was Michelangelo's favorite painter. Death came so suddenly that some believed Masaccio was poisoned.

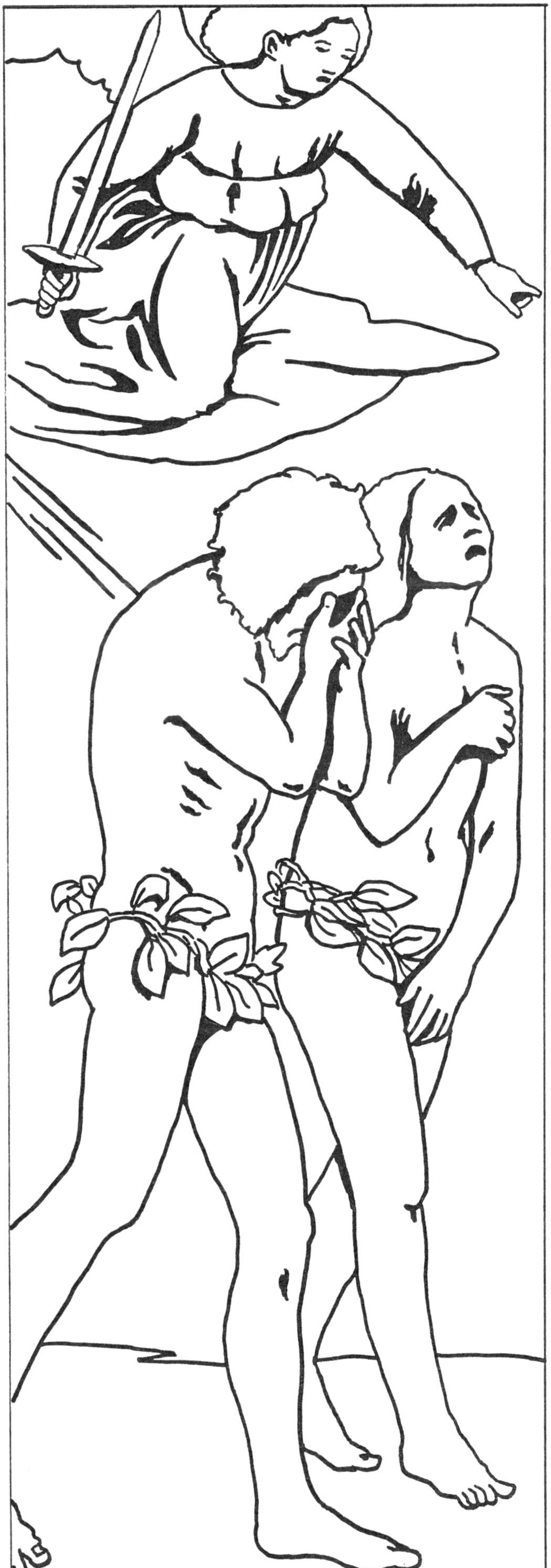

Fra Filippo Lippi (Fra Filippo di Tommasso, c. 1406–1469)

Tarquinia Madonna

Filippo Lippi was an orphan who lived a wild and adventurous life. After having taken a friar's vows, he left the monastery at fifteen; was held captive by Barbary pirates for eighteen months; and, at age fifty-one, ran away with a young novice who bore him a son, Filippino Lippi.

A·D·N·
CCCC·

PIERO DELLA FRANCESCA (born c. 1410–1420, died 1492)

The Nativity

This cobbler's son had first studied mathematics. In later life, upon suffering an artist's greatest tragedy—blindness—he published two very valuable books on mathematics. He died on October 12, 1492, just as Columbus was reaching the New World.

CASTAGNO (Andre del Castagna, 1423–1457)

The Youthful David

A peasant, orphaned at an early age, Castagna died of the plague at age thirty-four. For some time, history falsely accused him of murder. This image was painted on a leather shield used in processional parades. It can be seen in Washington's National Gallery.

CASTAGNO

The Cumaen Sibyl

Cumae was the earliest Greek colony in Italy. A sibyl was an ancient Greek or Roman woman—a fortune-teller or sorceress—who could prophesy under the influence of a deity. The Cumaeran Sibyl had nine books which revealed the destiny of Rome.

CVMANA OVE PROPHETAVIT ADVENTVM

MANTEGNA (Andrea Mantegna, c. 1431–1506)

Ascension (detail)

Mantegna was a humble field worker who rose to knighthood. He was an ingenious master of the foreshortened figure and an excellent copper engraver. Air raids in 1944 destroyed many of his frescoes in Padua but luckily photos had been taken just days before.

COSIMO TURA (c. 1432–1495)

Group of Horsemen

Cosimo Tura was a competent painter who made a lot of money from speculation. He is rumored to have become so wealthy that he once paid for the entire construction of a church. He was grateful to have achieved so much, this shoemaker's son.

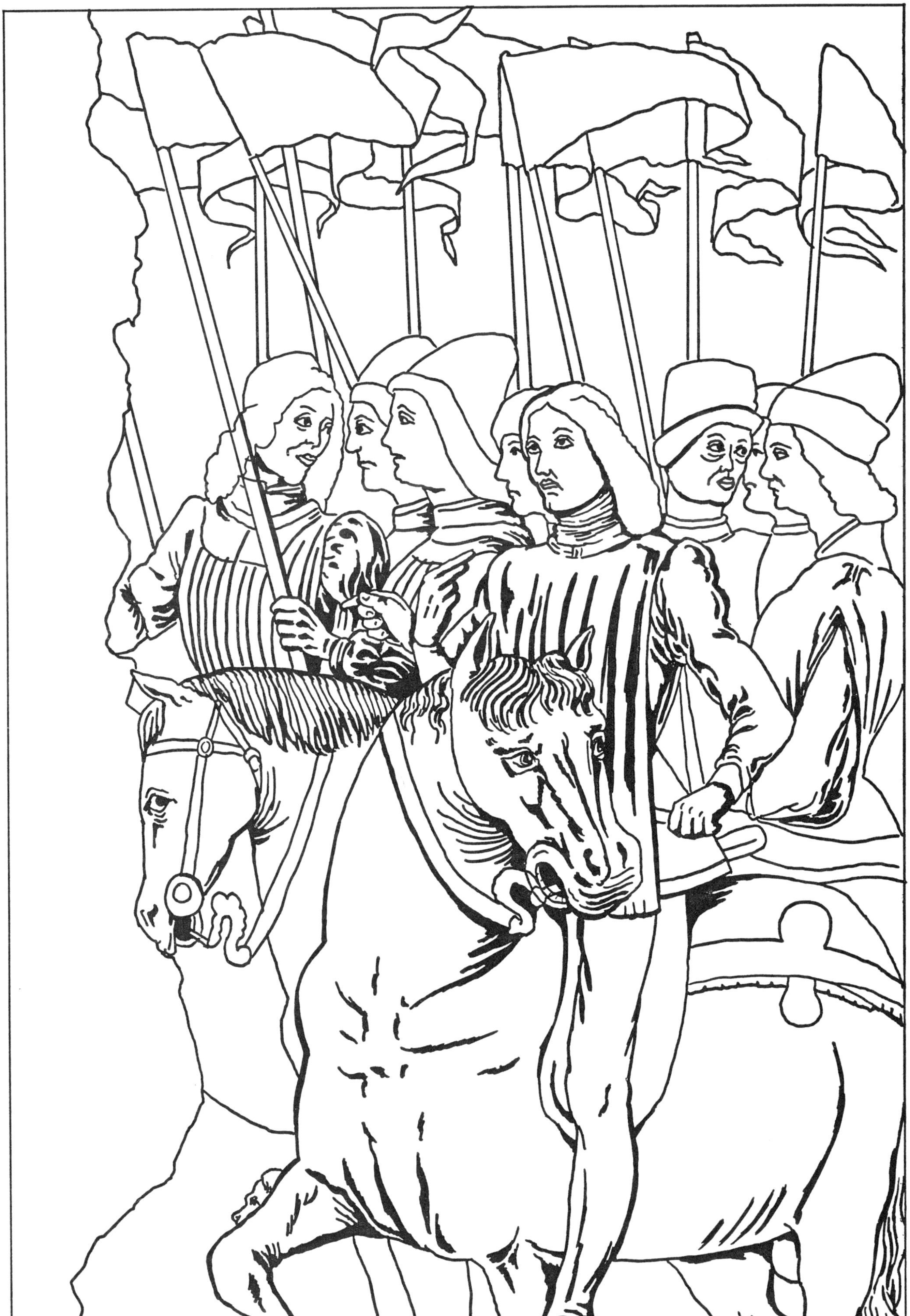

CARLO CRIVELLI (c. 1435–1493)

Virgin of the Passion (detail)

In 1547 Crivelli was sentenced to six months in prison for the kidnapping and restraint of a sailor's wife. Nevertheless, this transgression apparently did not prevent him from being knighted, due chiefly to his many political and military involvements.

VERROCHIO (Andrea del Verrochio, 1435–1488)

Tobias and the Angel

A far greater instructor than painter, Verrochio supposedly put down his brushes after recognizing the brilliance of his prize pupil, Leonardo. He also taught Ghirlandaio and Botticelli, and was considered the only sculptor who could rival Donatello.

MELOZZA DE FORLI (Marco degli Ambrosio, 1438–1494)

Angel Musician

Melozzo de Forli was a lesser-known artist who was greatly influenced by Piero della Francesca, whom he know personally. Melozzo was also a very close friend of Raphael's father, Giovanni Santi, who was also a painter.

BOTTICELLI (Alessandro di Mariano Filipepi/Sandro Botticelli, c. 1445–1510)

The Birth of Venus

Ironically, this painter of grace and beauty had the jovial personality of a practical joker. He made and misspent a lot of money before he died in poverty, supported by friends and patrons. This painting is quite large, measuring nearly 6x9 feet.

Botticelli

Pallas and the Centaur

Botticelli spent seven years in the studio of Fra Filippo Lippi. Upon his deathbed, Filippo Lippi asked a favor which Botticelli gladly granted. Botticelli was asked to educate the dying man's son, Fra Filippino Lippi, who also became a successful artist.

GHIRLANDAIO (Domenico di Tomaso Bigordi 1449–1494)

The Visitation

Ghirlandaio means "garland-maker": that was his father's profession. Ghirlandaio was Michelangelo's teacher. Later, these two artists, plus Botticelli, Raphael, and many, many others painted in the Sistine Chapel. *The Visitation* is in the Louvre.

Perugino (Vannucci Pietro, 1450–1524)

St. John the Evangelist and St. Augustine

Perugino, believed to be a classmate of Leonardo's under Verrochio, was himself the teacher of Raphael. Perugnio also painted at the Sistine Chapel, and as a city magistrate selected the site to place Michelangelo's sculpture, *David*. He died of the plague.

PINTURICCHIO (Bernadino de Betto, 1454–1513)

Portrait of a Young Boy

Pinturicchio, whose name means "the dauber in many colors," also painted at the Sistine Chapel, and was one of Raphael's closest friends. He was also called "Sordicchio" because he was a small, deaf man. Abandoned by his wife, he died of neglect at age fifty-nine.

LORENZO COSTA (c. 1460–1535)

The Ship of the Argonauts

Lorenzo Costa was a follower of the painter Cosimo Tura. Although he lived to an old age, it seems that very little of Costa's later work ever developed to any level beyond what he had already accomplished in his youth. That's a sad legacy for an artist to bear.

Piero di Cosimo (Piero di Lorenzo, c. 1462–1521)

The Madeleine

Born the son of a goldsmith, Piero di Cosimo worked at the Sistine Chapel as a painting assistant. Later he enjoyed success as an organizer of carnival festivities. He taught Andrea del Sarto—yet another example of the pupil outshining the teacher.

LEONARDO (Leonardo da Vinci, 1452–1519)

Last Supper (detail)

Seventeeth century monks knocked a doorway through Christ's legs in this 25′ long fresco at the Dominican Convent of Santa Maria delle Grazie, Milan. Napoleon's soldiers (against his wishes) used the room as a stable and threw darts at the heads of the apostles.

LEONARDO

Mona Lisa

Leonardo created few oil paintings, but this is the world's most famous. It's only 2′6″x 1′9″ but he worked on it four years before he was satisfied. Leonardo was the illegitimate son of a notary and a peasant girl. He and Michelangelo disliked each other intensely.

LEONARDO

Lady with a Jewel

Leonardo was an accomplished sculptor, goldsmith, engraver, architect, engineer, poet, philosopher, writer, inventor, musician, singer, mathematician, military strategist, and astronomer. No one since has equaled his combination of physical beauty, talent, and intelligence.

SOLARIO (Andrea Solario, c. 1460–1520)

Girl Playing a Lute

Solario came from a family of artists. He spent two years in France, painting a chapel which was destroyed in 1793. *Girl Playing a Lute* is a small oil painting on wood, only about 18x24 inches. It hangs in the Barberini Palace, Rome.

Fra Bartolomeo (Baccio della Porta, 1475–1517)

God Appearing to Saint Catherine and Saint Margaret

In 1497, Bartolomeo, Botticelli, and others, burned all their secular paintings in the "Bonfire of the Vanities." Three years later, a life-threatening incident prompted him to take a friar's vows. He was Raphael's best friend, and he died of a paralyzing stroke at forty-two

A ω

MICHELANGELO (Michelangelo Buonarroti, 1475–1564)

The Doni Madonna (detail)

Born to a prestigious family, Michelangelo's genius was considered equal to Leonardo's. More aggressive and dynamic than the elder da Vinci, Michelangelo was also a great poet, composing seventy-seven highly respected sonnets. This was his very first easel painting.

MICHELANGELO

God Creating Adam

His frescoes on the Sistine Chapel ceiling at the Vatican in Rome took four years, 1508–1512. At age sixty he returned to begin the 400 life-size figures for *The Last Judgement* on the Chapel wall: He was sixty-six when he finished them. His closest friend was writer Giorgio Vasari.

MICHELANGELO

The Conversion of Saint Paul (detail)

Temperamental, small, and homely, with a severely broken nose, Michelangelo was the physical and emotional opposite of his two rivals, Leonardo and Raphael. He spent the last seventeen years of his life designing the architecture for St. Peter's Cathedral in Rome.

BERNARDINO LUINI (c. 1480–1532)

The Deliverance of the Israelites

Luini never set foot outside Italy. He was twice unlucky in love: A patron's daughter whom he loved was sent to a nunnery; later, he allegedly committed murder for love. Finally he married, fathering a daughter, and two sons who painted at his side.

GAUDENZIO FERRARI (c. 1484–1546)

Angel Musicians

Gaudenzio Ferrari was a close friend of Bernadino Luini. His paintings were greatly influenced by Raphael. Ferrari's most famous masterpiece is the 21-panel *Life of Christ* in Verallo, Italy. Some believe that Ferrari and Luini were pupils of Leonardo.

Andrea del Sarto (Andrea d'Agnolosi, c. 1486–1531)

Abraham's Sacrifice

A goldsmith, engraver, and painter, Andrea was nicknamed "del Sarto" because his father was a tailor. He spent a year as a guest painter at Fontainebleau Palace in France at the invitation of King Francis I. His major work, *The Life of John the Baptist,* took fifteen years.

TITIAN (Tiziano Vecelli, c. 1477–1576)

Isabella d'Este, Margrave of Manuta

The son of an important lawyer, Titian painted for popes and kings for over seventy years! At age seventy-one, he crossed the Alps during winter to paint two portraits of his beloved friend, Charles V, King of Spain. Titian painted his last masterpiece, *Pieta*, at the age of ninety-nine!

TITIAN

Don Fernando Alvarez di Toledo, Grand-Duke of Alba

So revered was Titian that when he died of the plague shortly before his 100th birthday, the Venetian Senate made an exception to the law that the bodies of all plague victims must be burned and ordered the great artist's remains interred instead.

RAPHAEL (Raffaello Santi or Sanzio, 1483–1520)

St. George Slaying the Dragon

This tiny (about 10x12 inch) oil painting on wood was commissioned as a gift for King Henry VIII of England. Later owners included King Charles I of Great Britain and Ireland, and Catherine the Great, Empress of Russia. Today, it hangs in the Louvre.

Raphael

The Madonna of the Chair

Raphael painted more than twenty Madonnas. His own mother died when Raphael was only eight. His father (painter Giovanni Santi) died three years later, so the young orphan was raised by uncles. He was a small boy, but extremely handsome and intelligent.

RAPHAEL

Galatea

The charming and personable Raphael was a friend to all who met him.
The only exception was Michelangelo, whose popularity the younger artist, Raphael, challenged.
The German artist Albrecht Dürer visited Italy twice and sought out Raphael's friendship.

Raphael

The Vision of Ezekiel

A favorite of popes, Raphael painted at the Sistine Chapel and designed Vatican tapestries. He was also placed in charge of Rome's ancient buildings, overseeing all excavations in the city. This work, like *The Madonna of the Chairs,* hangs in Florence's Pitti Palace.

RAPHAEL

Portrait of a Young Woman

This painting, created in 1505–06, is also known as *The Lady of the Unicorn*. Raphael died of exhaustion at the young age of thirty-seven. Often overlooked among the many achievements of his noteworthy career is the fact that he also trained more than fifty aspiring young painters.

BRONZINO (Angelo di Cosimo, 1502–1572)

Portrait of Guidobaldo della Rovere

Nicknamed "Bronzino" for his dark complexion, this artist came from a poor family. He, like Michelangelo, was an intimate friend of the art historian Giorgio Vasari. Bronzino's skills earned him the coveted position of official portrait painter to the Medici family.

Sofinisha Anguissola (1531–1625)

Lucia, Minerva, and Europa Anguissola Playing Chess

In 1555, when Bronzino was fifty-three, Titian was sixty-eight, Michelangelo was eighty, and all other Renaissance painters had been dead for twenty years, this painting was created by twenty-four-year-old Sofinisha Anguissola, the first Italian woman to gain international fame as an artist.

Other Culpepper Press Coloring Books

The Impressionists Coloring Book
By Andy Nelson
ISBN 0-929636-06-6
$5.95 96 pp 48 drawings

The Carl Larsson Coloring Book
By Andy Nelson
ISBN 0-929636-07-4
$5.95 96 pp 45 drawings

To purchase additional Culpepper Press coloring books ask your local bookstore to order it for you or send $5.95 per copy plus $1.75 shipping and handling per order to: Culpepper Press, 6921 Gordan Road, Siren, WI 54872.